I0840964

DAFT LEFT

by Karen Kellock Ph.D.

Manual for
Superior Men

A complete theory based on Einstein physics,
Political Psychology, Systems Theory
and Archetypal Psychiatry.

FORMULA

All success attraction
All disease obstruction
All recovery elimination

You must fast on all three

OBSTRUCTIONS:

People
Habit
Food

DAFT LEFT

It's a painful thing being a stranger in a strange land filled with false accusations.   It's part of the path because you're growing and they're not: a time of misperception/feeling left out for it's a severe eruption as homeostasis is maintained.   The worse their portrayal of you then the more miraculous your recovery now friend.   When the appetite [desire] rules we make huge mistakes: this is the rule for the saints.

IT'S SATAN LASHING OUT

THEY TEAM UP AGAINST YOU
CLEAN SWEEP
DON'T LET EM IN YOUR HOUSE
SATAN'S THE AUTHOR OF CONFUSION
PEOPLE ARE JEALOUS OF YOU
DON'T TOLERATE CONFUSION
DON'T BRING OLD SPIRITS BACK
SATAN PULLS DOWN YOUR ENERGY
LET GO OF PEOPLE/PLACES/THINGS
STEP INTO YOUR GIFT
HOLY SEPARATION TO WORK
BE A TARGET FOR MEN'S SOULS
I JUST WANTED TO BE ALONE
ENTIRELY DIFFERENT FROM THEM
THIS JOURNEY IS FRUSTRATING
USE FRUSTRATION IN THE GYM
WHEN THE SNAKES CIRCLE BACK
CHOSENS DESERVE SUCCESS
LIGHT SURROUNDED BY DARKNESS
THE WELL-KNOWN UNKNOWN
GLOW OF THE HOLY SPIRIT
AVOID EYE CONTACT FIRST
PRAYER PROTECTS FROM DEMONS
DON'T LET OBSESSED IN YOUR HOME

IT'S SATAN LASHING OUT

THEY TEAM UP AGAINST YOU

They gang-stalk and team up against you. The chosen must be ready for that, it's a promise too.

The left is so social, it's all about collusion and mobbing you. The right is independent, we're the cool.

The devil is the author of confusion. He LOVES division and them gossiin'. So hang on to God son.

When even strangers lash out at you it's the devil. It's a spiritual battle and for the chosen it's predictable.

Satan will do anything in his power to provoke your spirit and it only comes thru people, know it.

The reason so much hell is thrown at you is cuz you gotta let people go for good--more than a few.

Ever since you started living for Jesus as He did a new thing in you, you're a threat to the world too.

As you rise up in new status the devil is mad. That's the reason for the armor of God that you have.

Yes you gotta be done with old friends, soul ties and the memory of them as well. You've been thru hell.

Tho' old habits & addictions are gone some remnants remain and you need a clean sweep son.

CLEAN SWEEP

IT'S SATAN LASHING OUT

Out with old relationships who did you no good. Then God brings in new friends, well understood.

The devil's trying to distract you and that's why you gotta be done with people for good Sue.

Clean out your whole house, every drawer. God wants you to rid old spirits out of cars and more.

The past must be wiped out completely. God's doing a new thing in you so gotta let the old go see.

DON'T LET EM IN YOUR HOUSE

Above all, don't let people into your house. It's a sacred place just for you not spirits in that louse.

After all that cleansing, PTSD remains. I understand that friends, it's hard ridding memories ok.

Everyone tried to hold you back. Block you, stop you or swapping destinies with you was a daily fact.

This is a new beginnings day so don't be afraid to wipe out old contacts/totally reject.

People not supporting you and never checking on you: wipe out old contacts from your phone too.

You're a totally new person now so all old contacts are not suitable, dangerous or downright low.

SATAN'S THE AUTHOR OF CONFUSION

The devil's the author of confusion. He loves division and disagreements and triggering you son.

IT'S SATAN LASHING OUT

You get used to things like people dropping in and in so doing lose your own spirit and reality friends.

I thought I'd lose my mind from the confusion people brought in. All in the name of good, amen.

Satan throws many demonic spirits at you because he knows you're just that powerful and true.

God's giving a new anointing so you gotta let people go for good & don't let em back in, understood?

PEOPLE ARE JEALOUS OF YOU

People have been jealous of you, hatin' & plottin' against you all along and now they're back on?

It seems like every time you come to a new level here comes chaos, confusion, some new division.

The devil is a liar. They're accusing of something you didn't even do, never think of or even conspire.

Let go of all old friends and soul ties then "remember them no more". Sink em good then soar.

Plant your feet on high ground boy and send em away at the same time. Do it now, sink the crap, aye!

DON'T TOLERATE CONFUSION

Every time God tries to send confusion away you pulled em back to be nice or for nostalgia's sake.

Memories of the blokes are spirits too. The whole past remnant must be gone so work on it Sue.

IT'S SATAN LASHING OUT

Every time God elevates you expect the enemy to come at you. That's the way it works so prepare Sue.

Because God will always fight your battles, the more the enemy attacks the more God will bless you.

You have a whole new life and spirit. God's given you a career and money so why ever go back to it.

There's gonna always be some kind of attack cuz you have God in you so learn to stand tall Sue.

DON'T BRING OLD SPIRITS BACK

Don't you ever bring those old spirits back in cuz God's giving you everything NEW now friends.

When Satan sends his gangsalkers your way--chains of confusion--know it's just a test & new level ok.

God gives many breakthroughs--not just one--so we gotta pass many tests: it's about self-respect.

People are fighting demonic spirits each and every day so you gotta learn to STAY OUT THE WAY.

Rmember friend: the bigger the attack the bigger the blessing but you've got armor for self-protecting.

SATAN PULLS DOWN YOUR ENERGY

Satan. It feels like someone's pulling on your energy: stalking you and following you all around see.

You're the chosen one so they want some of that energy off of you but self-respect controls that Sue.

IT'S SATAN LASHING OUT

It's a funny thing but cuz you pulled em outa that storm they feel they own you now. They're dumb cows.

Cut off the things creating noise. The confusion is building up from Satan but you have choice.

Cut off things that are trying to provoke your spirit. You wake up angry: you know it and can feel it.

LET GO OF PEOPLE/PLACES/THINGS

You gotta let go of people, places & things. Listen to me man: it's where angels fear to tread, amen.

Stop fighting their battles, being a peacemaker or a silly tolerator to be "nice": you're not mice.

You can't be the peacemaker to other's problems cuz that's how Satan's trying to destroy you man.

If in the middle of things they'll turn around and accuse you for it. It's what happens with involvements.

We give our lives to God. We give Him the glory, He gives us the victory. That's how it is done.

Women today don't know how to treat a king because they're not a queen. It's as simple ss that see.

STEP INTO YOUR GIFT

The answer is to step into your gift because that won't abandon you for your whole life, promised.

As long as you have a purpose and your own kick ass life things won't go wrong: stand tall alone.

IT'S SATAN LASHING OUT

Stay in your own power **THEN** you can support others. You've been troubled doing things backwards.

Many women suck men into their false fantasy world. They'll drive you friggin' crazy these girls.

There's a power dynamic and one always has more, thus laying the groundwork for cruelties galore.

Whoever's most rare has more power. They have it in abundance cuz they worked every day/hour.

As your power rises--cuza what you've done--you see a massive difference in how you're treated hon'.

A woman who preserves herself is far more respected than anyone. It's not work just holy restriction.

HOLY SEPARATION TO WORK

Become the man or woman you're supposed to be and you'll have the pick of the litter/all options see.

Men going their own way for the simple fact that's the only way to go. They go high, women go low.

MGTOW should have happened back in the seventies when women decided not to be true ladies.

Things got into men's heads due to sex and they stopped believing who they were: a hex.

If surrounded by the wrong things it gets in your head and you forget who you are or go bad instead.

Modern kids think they're cool but they're all losers. They don't do the work or postpone pleasures.

So you're all alone. I'm here, and I'm happily alone. It's all how you think about things high or low.

IT'S SATAN LASHING OUT

If you have a weak mind you'll have a weak life. It's all in your mind whether grateful or in strife.

Be cautious and unmovable cuz spirits are around and when it happens, stand your ground.

You gotta be FIRM in your assignment, no matter what. That's the only buffer against attacks & nuts.

BE A TARGET FOR MEN'S SOULS

Ask God to make you a great target for men's souls. For His kingdom only not for demons of old.

The devil's constantly throwing old soul tie distractions back in your life, that's why you feel strife.

Things happening decades back, even tho' the actors are long gone or dead: and you're a sad sack?

Satan throws darts all day long--of anxiety, depression, oppression--but God protects you all along.

If God be fore you, who can be against you? No matter what you feel come back to that vital truth.

You may have to live years in a bed of isolation for there's nothing worse than the wrong people son.

Having unwanted people around you can build tremendous resentment. I know it cuz I've had it.

I JUST WANTED TO BE ALONE

I just wanted to work & think, study & ruminate, look out the window & cogitate while they'd irritate.

Being around people who are not good for you and hold you back will make you crazy and lazy in fact.

IT'S SATAN LASHING OUT

I still recall the frustration of being around losers who would not leave me alone many decades ago.

Being around inappropriate people will stunt your growth more than you'll ever know: it's the foe.

For growth you need positive momentum in your life, not losers and screwups. It's essential bud.

You can have a normal life just don't get close. It's too toxic and it doesn't take much to curse it.

ENTIRELY DIFFERENT FROM THEM

You're on an entirely different level. I became so prickly I felt crazy like an elder dog with a jittery puppy.

If stuck with people who aren't growing themselves they'll trap you. You'll be stuck/feel screwed.

They want you stuck down with them, but is that what you want? Not: you want to get to the top.

On this journey, resentment is going to build. You'll feel frustrated and irritated in a kind of grey hell.

People ain't like you and you ain't like people cuz you are chosen by God. State this fact out loud!

"Why can't you be like everyone else?" my aunt would say. As if I had a choice or could be a fake.

The devil had them in a stranglehold but you fought your way outa that tooth and nail, bold.

THIS JOURNEY IS FRUSTRATING

The journey is frustrating so we take that energy and hone it in: use it for something good friend.

IT'S SATAN LASHING OUT

If you channel your energy you'll be better than 99% of people on earth. This really makes you superior.

You gotta realize you live a completely different lifestyle. How different you are is light years and miles.

They pooh-pooh money as if it's a curse but meanwhile mooch off of you: that's the crazy new agers.

USE FRUSTRATION IN THE GYM

Take that frustration and go to the gym or on a run. Don't let anxiety build, you know it's no fun.

You're allowed to have those feelings but it's up to you what you do about em through channeling.

When you redirect those feelings you realize YOU'RE in control and it's a helluva sense, it's monumental.

In stress we get in our own way. Now we must take power to get out of our way and go forward ok.

Stay strong and make hard decisions even when you don't feel like it. This is your key or forget it.

The weatherman's not in control, he says rain. It's YOU in control no matter what, that's the king ok.

WHEN THE SNAKES CIRCLE BACK

Women vastly underestimate the work it takes to have relationship yet press for commitment anyway.

Getting a man and keeping him are two totally different things but you can't see that darling.

"I can't get a man to commit", "modern men are noncommittal", "they're all pigs don't you know?

IT'S SATAN LASHING OUT

Most modern women today are unaccountable and won't own their own actions or behavior at all.

I was scammed by a lady and instead of admitting it she'd deflect to how nice she'd been to me.

Now when the snakes circle back be ready and keep em out, they're crap. Now you'll be a success Mack!

When you're chosen by God there's gonna be jealousy & hatred coming to you while the angels applaud.

Let the frenemy scammer go but also everyone who dared to justify her for they're just as bad sir.

Be careful who you trust out there for the true are few. And when you sense deception avoid em sue.

People come in one way and end totally different. You gotta pick up on cues and then that's it.

CHOSENS DESERVE SUCCESS

You can't trust anyone. They come into your life with a full mask on so get your radar up & keep it up hon'.

After all you've been thru you DESERVE success. I want you to know that, it's crucial to see that sis.

You've been scapegoated and railroaded, interrupted constantly and invaded--now be rewarded.

They lied on you and teamed up against you. They spread untrue stories and hated you too.

The stress they put you through was more than anyone could take but you took it and overcame it ok.

If anyone has ever deserved success, it is YOU. You must see that and congratulate yourself too.

IT'S SATAN LASHING OUT

You've been thru the misery experienced by all chosens: to be hated, targeted and scapegoated, amen.

Your own family lied on you and spread stories around. You didn't have a fighting chance being so bound.

Everyone figured if your family said it it must be true, so you didn't have a chance when defending you.

Everyone figured your older sister knew the scoop so any self-defense was regarded as just poop.

You've been thru the ringer so simply put: you deserve success and God will grant you magic luck.

LIGHT SURROUNDED BY DARKNESS

The gangstalkers are so obsessed with you. Can't a chosen get some space? It's so irritating/uncool.

You are the light surrounded by darkness. They are drawn to you like it's a matter of survival sis.

They follow you cuz they've never seen someone like you before. They've been in the dark for sure.

When you're chosen/made in the image of God everywhere you go they'll be drawn/awed.

When you're the light surrounded by darkness the vibrancy captivates and attracts them see.

The result of thsi mass attraction is the utter lack of privacy and it's enough to drive you crazy.

God has elevated us in the spiritual realm so we don't even show that we've been through hell.

We have a new level of anointing as the holy spirit's in us. They see this bright/fascinating difference.

IT'S SATAN LASHING OUT

We are earth angels and that's why people stalk us. I literally had to relocate to get privacy sis.

You're peaceful, gentle, loving and kind. People see the difference and just wanna be with you, aye.

THE WELL-KNOWN UNKNOWN

You're the well-known unknown just by your aura and divine presence. You're known in silence.

The chosen don't hang out in packs or groups. That's one way you're known you're chosen Sue.

We don't hang around low vibrational entities and it's pure torture when they get thru to us see.

God is continually taking you higher and higher in life until mass attractions reach a pitch, aye.

People gangstalk cuz there's something different about you. Obsession can be a bad thing, even cruel.

When people are obsessed they'll do anything to get your attention and get mad when they can't son.

GLOW OF THE HOLY SPIRIT

You have a glow of the holy spirit and it's blinding to them. You gotta hide to get any space son.

When they're constantly staring and you look away they get mad because they can't have access ok.

They want access to your spirit but you can't allow it. It's a sensitive situation, you'd better know it.

You must know how valuable you are so stop giving people you info. Get off of social media too.

IT'S SATAN LASHING OUT

You are a rare commodity: unusual and special. So don't let down your guard ever and at all.

Once you shut em out of your presence [can't get a piece of you] you see what they're all about too.

You come into a presence sensing a demonic spirit on the attack. You can't even make eye contact.

AVOID EYE CONTACT FIRST

Since the eyes are the windows to the soul you can't even make eye contact anymore that's all.

Eye contact means your holy spirit confronts their demons so you can't even do that man.

Thus you need the full armor of God to protect from the fiery darts of the devil: and the deeply flawed.

And thus the saints pray constantly. For the more we pray the more power God gives for safety.

When you pray and venture out to the real world you feel at peace as if angels are guarding see.

As you pray God reveals the gangstalkers and you will see even your own neighbors and sisters.

When you talk to neighbors you sense a spirit that is low vibrational and you wanna go home that's. all.

PRAYER PROTECTS FROM DEMONS

Thru prayer God will protect you from seen and unseen dangers. Stay sober and you'll always be secure.

As God gives you more power and gifts these people will be coming from all directions, so resist.

IT'S SATAN LASHING OUT

You must be careful and prayerful. Obsessions were a scary thing to me till I saw God was her now.

God will give you the POWER of love and a sound mind. Keep your private safe space and be humble/kind.

As a chosen you're hypersensitive to energy and when it's that bad you gotta walk away fast see.

DON'T LET OBSESSED IN YOUR HOME

They're so obsessed you don't dare let em in your house. You are the light & they are darkness.

Because you are the light you will attract demonic spirits. They want you down, it's just how it is.

Because you're chosen they'll either want your autograph or praise God want to be saved ok.

Your intuition is your best friend and it's the holy spirit. You know all about a person so listen to it.

Your intuition is God. He leads and guides you, He warns you and goads you even thru His rod.

THE LEFT MADE ME SICK

LOVE GOD FIRST NOT PEOPLE
FIRST THEY LOVE YOU, THEN...
DANGEROUS OLD WOMEN
IS ISOLATION THE ONLY SOLUTION?

THE LEFT MADE ME SICK

LOVE GOD FIRST NOT PEOPLE

People aren't that important so don't make em or life will turn tragic. God first then life is magic.

They betrayed me so much with hurts it acted as a python squeezing out 90,000 proverbs.

I have no more adversaries because I saw them all, relocated to Utah and then built a wall.

The Jews were beaten in the streets: by neighbors and even children, not soldiers or the Nazis.

They love getting wind on someone who's "bad" so they can blamelessly commit violent acts.

When I was down/out I saw the wild wickedness of people esp. from friends/relatives gone evil.

When you're down they treat you like shit and tell their circle to do the same, inviting em to it.

I know they're friends and family but watch out for people just the same--they can all turn today.

FIRST THEY LOVE YOU, THEN...

This isn't the fifties with big loving families. We're all atomized now and brainwashed with inanities.

Scapegoatism is BIG with adulterous generations of the latter day, sinners are mean ok.

In order to round up and kill six million Jews the Nazis had already made people hate them too.

THE LEFT MADE ME SICK

First they love you then they talk to someone else and they hate you: they're socially driven Sue.

Never get sucked into their reality about you. You'll be filled with self-disgust & failure if you do.

If your tribe hates you as horrible it's hard to think you're great but that's the test mate.

People just love to turn on someone, it scratches an itch going way back to paleo times son.

When sisters go along with your alcoholic husband who hates you life can turn very cruel.

You go along with their nonsense or you're out then suffer for years with rejection and pout.

DANGEROUS OLD WOMEN

Some purify with age, others get more evil at each stage. Don't assume a thing, that's ageist.

The old women were all alike and I grew terrified of them so socially-driven, to my ruination.

As a creative artist so independent they had a problem with that and tried to MAKE me adapt.

They were mean old bitties and dangerous gossips. Innuendoes and sly accusations are tragic.

The old bitties are shrewish and nagging: life is sad and hellish if you're the one they're targeting.

Every old bittie I clashed with in that dark era became a terrible foe while "helping" ya know.

THE LEFT MADE ME SICK

They're always stirring up trouble, always on the horn cuz that's how they manage: thru lore.

Latter Days: with more time on their hands women made dangerous enemies: treachery.

You got the old bitties who are treacherous and the young bitties who are promiscuous.

They hate her cuz she doesn't look like them, doesn't react or talk like them-- that's all friend.

An old bittie can leave you with a self-disgust complex and it can go on for decades like a hex.

IS ISOLATION THE ONLY SOLUTION?

Not wanting to deal with people's mean projections puts you in isolation but that's ok son.

How can you concentrate/focus on something when expected to be social? You can't ya know.

Being oppressed by foes gave me a deeper/more authentic knowledge of life and society.

Black women are new gunowners in democrat cities, knowing they must protect themselves see.

Deep State Siege: by making us poor they can dictate the terms of our unconditional surrender.

This is the greatest advice I can have for you: never travel to El Salvador if you have a tattoo.

Lost his wife: so overtaken with grief he sunk in his swill and wanted to die/couldn't wait until.

Before He rewards us God must test us. That may account for all your trouble lately sis.

THE LEFT MADE ME SICK

"We like being together but we like solitude even better" said the happily married partner.

After becoming what he allowed he rejected her and she sunk in her swill until she saw God.

The main problem with wife of alcoholic is no one believes her, he's a mildly soused critic.

The church should not be downstream from culture. Wearing jeans, tattoos or hats in church.

Reading dictionary pages works just as good as a Tarot readout: uncanny for synchronicity nuts.

Taking instruction is a left brain thing and I just can't do it anymore said an artist while retiring.

Leave the Land of Lack. If you want two houses you can have two even though most do not.

DAFT LEFT

SINGLE IS A RUDDERLESS SHIP
DO YOUR WORK OR SMERK CURSE
MENTAL ILLNESS AND MARRIAGE
NO MORE RESTRAINT
TAKING ON THE BAD IDENTITY
REPENTANCE PURIFIES THE PAST
FALSE ACCUSATION AND MISJUDGEMENT
EVERYTHING IS TURNED AROUND
THE NEED FOR VIGILANCE
DEBASED SPOUSES ARE EMPTY VESSELS
AGING INTO BEAUTIFUL WHOLES
INNER CRITICS ARE OLD BASHERS
HATRED OF SUPERIORITY: REGICIDE
FEMINISM IS A SEVERE UNDERTOW
LIMITLESS EVIL IN THE PEOPLE
YOUR HOME IS YOUR KINGDOM
DOUBLETHINK IS NEVER TRUE
WISE TO SUBTLE SABOTAGE
PSYCHOTIC TYRANTS IN HISTORY
IT'S HOW THE SYSTEM DIVIDES THINGS
SYSTEMS OF CONSTANT TERROR
HATRED AND ENVY IS HUMAN SOCIETY
LIVING WITH THE DUMBED
HOW TO MAKE GOLD
LESSONS LEARNED WHEN YOUNG
SOUL TIES ARE NOT LOVE
PREJUDICE IS PROGRESSIVE
BASHED STEREOTYPES
MALICIOUS PEOPLE DON'T CHANGE
LUKEWARM CHRISTIAN SIBLINGS

DAFT LEFT

GO GREY ROCK
EDUCATE GIRLS ON PSYCHOPATHS
TERRIFYING RELATIONSHIPS
SICK WITH FEAR AND PANIC
DARK AND MENACING PRESENCE
CULTURE TEACHES MENTAL ILLNESS
TOXIC SHAME PASSED DOWN
SILENT CLUB OF SUPERIORITY
MOST WRONG BECOMES MOST RIGHT
ARCHETYPES POSITIVE AND NEGATIVE
REAL MEN ARE CONSERVATIVE
POLITICS SPLITS THE HICKS
IDENTITY STRUGGLES AND BOOZE
EVIL RISES UP THEN SO DOES GOOD
SEXUALIZE AND BRAIN DAMAGE KIDS
BRAINLESS VIRTUE SIGNALING
UGLINESS FROM LEFTIST DESIGNERS
HOLLYWOOD SCUM ATTACKS TRUMP
HANKERING FOR THE DEAD PAST
GET BUSY AND DO YOUR THING
HOLLYWOOD IS EXTENSION OF DEMS
BLATANT HYPOCRASY OF MEDIA NEWS
HOLLYWOOD FAKE THUGS: EMINEM
FREEDOM IS SEXIEST
IN HOLLYWOOD RAPE IS OK IF IT'S GAY
EMMYS ARE A BASH-TRUMPFEST
RINOS AND NEOCONS JUST AS BAD
DEMOCRATS RUINED CITIES FOR 100 YEARS
LIBERAL PSYCHOLOGIST SCAM

DAFT LEFT

HEF EMPOWERED WOMEN TO BE VERMIN
CULTURE IS INTRIGUE, WISDOM, BEAUTY
POPULAR CULTURE IS VULGAR
HIP HOP AND ISLAM IN YOUNG MEN
TRUMP RESPECTS WOMEN
THE COASTS ARE EVIL DEM STRONGHOLDS
DEPLORABLES ARE >HALF THE COUNTRY
OLD RAPPERS NEED CIVICS
THEY'RE CRUDE AND RUDE
THEY'RE PAID TO BRAINWASH US
AMERICA'S COMING BACK
HARVEY AND BILL BUILT A PORN ROOM
OBAMA SET THE PRECEDENT
WATCH FOR EVIL CLOWNS
AND WE THOUGHT CARTER WAS BAD
LEFT WANTS NO-GOD AND HUGE GOV
THEY CAN'T STAND US WINNING
DUMBED BY DOGMA
VIOLENCE AGAINST US IS LEGIT
SELF-DEFENSE MECHANISMS AND CONSCIENCE
MANUAL UNLEARNS DEMORALIZATION
FAKE RUSSIAN COLLUSION IS ALL THEY HAVE
TRUMP RANG MY BELL—SAVE US FROM HELL!
PEDOPHILIA REFLECTS ABORTION CULTURE
UNDERSTANDING LOST IN LOGORHEA (MANY WORDS)
CONSERVATIVES SEE THROUGH
GOVERNMENT THE DANGEROUS MASTER
BODY OF A JOCKEY
DAILY FASTING IS NOT ANOREXIA

DAFT LEFT

The worse their portrayal of you back then the more miraculous your recovery now my friend.

When the appetite [desire] rules we make huge mistakes. This is the rule for the saints.

Despite your sinning they always saw the genius of the situation so don't worry man, keep movin'.

Things happen like Nazi Germany and the buildup is fast. Learn of politics, for survival you must.

To champs: It was a horrible thing being a stranger in a strange land filled with false accusations.

It's part of the path because you're growing and they're not--a time of misperception/feeling left out.

It's a severe disjuncture in a system sure to cause eruption as homeostasis is maintained son.

If the only way to maintain the system is to trip yourself up that's what you'll be doin' until then.

SINGLE IS A RUDDERLESS SHIP

A single woman can't be a rudderless ship lest life turn to shit. She must be stronger/morally fit.

It was scary because i knew they couldn't understand me due to the Dunning-Kruger Effect see.

But as a single woman who was different and way out there, the looky loos would drive by in cars.

DAFT LEFT

I literally had to get married to get people to stop bothering me: provision and protection see.

A single woman has a bull's eye painted on her. I found that out in a small town years before.

They don't care if you're getting ahead now. You were their supply for a time and now you're gone.

Stop with the guilt and shame thing cuz you've an abnormal amount of it after repentance.

DO YOUR WORK OR SMERK CURSE

Discoveries like in the Renaissance are no longer made cuz people are derailed by their appetites.

A true Creative Act takes decades like Mt. Rushmore or this--who's gonna do all that nowadays?

It's all bravado, descriptions of self/talent, selfies, promotions but no a real Creative Act.

Tho' she drove & belittled to make you a better person she also traumatized you for no reason.

One may think I had privacy way out there but when the wolves came I was up a creek and scared.

All that matters is to me a lady is that my husband loves me so you can go straight to hell buddy.

He died the same way as friend. Sober, it had progressed = when he drank again, the end.

MENTAL ILLNESS AND MARRIAGE

Mental illness is a terrible thing. It is triggered by getting married or quickly healed by the same.

DAFT LEFT

Why come to Johnny's defense? He's an addict and that's how it had progressed, that's it.

Ravenous wolves, that's what they were. Blaming me for what THEY did, wanted or preferred.

Not until my PTSD lifted did I realize how dangerous you were. Up til then I was in denial for sure.

For I see now there is NOTHING you won't do—a loose canon, a rudderless ship and empty twit.

For very few now have Christian restraint and wild pugnacity is actually the accepted way.

So if your aggressiveness is accepted that means I must relocate now to escape who knows what.

If rather than confronting their invasion they question your desire to be alone, relocate NOW.

NO MORE RESTRAINT

There is no more restraint. People give us their bad side and it's tough but in marriage there's escape.

If they're all mean and nasty esp the women then the civilization is going into judgement and ruin.

God wants you to have a happy life, not wallowing in the filth he saved you from—that's disrespect hon'.

The worse you were & the more they gossiped about you the bigger they look as a fool now.

God said His elect shall not be condemned. It's who we are now not back then so let it go friend.

It was the Dunning-Kruger Effect of the dumb judging God's elect and it seemed insolvable/a hex.

DAFT LEFT

They knew nothing but that I was different from them and that's all they needed to persecute.

TAKING ON THE BAD IDENTITY

My problem was taking on the bad identity pasted on me. It took years on the Potter's wheel see.

Once they've laid that bad rap on you I say forgive em but don't see em again/don't go back in.

They don't care if you're a world success all they know is: you're not their supply anymore miss.

I never knew people could go that low. Humans are a bottomless pit when it comes to evil.

He was drunk from the time he got up to when he went to bed but the world judged me instead.

Since you shall not be condemned their words shall be because there is no time nor space see.

REPENTANCE PURIFIES THE PAST

When God purifies you He purifies the past too so now you'll have pleasant memories come thru.

A small town with people who didn't understand me and you set em off with your lies/inciting riots.

Every woman in Al-Anon understands Amber heard but the pro-Johnny world blames her.

Until you've lived with a dam alcoholic you have no idea what Amber Heard went thru: horrific.

Her gossiping all over town--laying evil seeds against you--was like getting a bunch of hitmen.

DAFT LEFT

It's not Johnny it's his disease and his wife had to deal with that--alcohol's a conduit to the devil.

FALSE ACCUSATION AND MISJUDGEMENT

My season of treason was a period of false accusation and misjudgment and it was hellish man.

They spread it around and file it away. They get a bee in their bonnet and then mob you that day.

See that little lady there? You think she's innocent but she's like a scorpion in her malicious gossipin'.

I take exception to the systems-theoretic view that no one is to blame--there IS a victim here ok.

EVERYTHING IS TURNED AROUND

They wanna turn everything around justified by early trauma and hate her as the evil momma.

Since alcohol is a conduit to the devil living with one is below hell as the wife's spirit is made small.

If you're something they can't understand they'll always peg you in a lower archetype--sorry man.

Only when the last brick of the building goes in do you attract the link [of completion] to the seed.

Systems Theory: there are no victims or culprits. The truth, reality: there IS a victim & dam brats.

Narcissists will always bust boundaries the minute you lay them--e.g. office hours and your husband.

Only when complete does the seed attract the link: a very nifty insight as we near the end see.

DAFT LEFT

Why you feel shame, guilt, invaded, belittled and blamed: it's the Mother Wound mate.

THE NEED FOR VIGILANCE

Your only problem is you should be more afraid of people. Be firm and boundaried against evil.

I take exception to the systems-theoretic view that she brought on his porn-- she's a victim too.

When the devil's the default setting all kinds of things can happen, the carrier's a loose canon.

DEBASED SPOUSES ARE EMPTY VESSELS

The wife of the alcoholic is so debased she may walk around like an empty vessel for decades.

The desire to eat everything in sight: an obvious sign of trauma then he's hooked by taste/aromas.

The allergy takes over and the alcoholic targets his own spouse, degrading her into mental illness.

You get visions of a prior self and then get anxious and riled up--replace memories to make it stop.

Women who hate Amber have low self-esteem. Out of pure jealousy they wish to topple a queen.

It was always me trying but unable to explain myself. That was the Dunning-Kruger dumb hell.

I want to create, you wanna bloviate. That's the difference between you and me mate.

AGING INTO BEAUTIFUL WHOLES

They see aging as running out of parts not completion of more meaningful wholes and rare arts.

DAFT LEFT

The gist: He drew me into his mental illness, I drew him into my addiction and ancillary craziness.

The purer you are the more bad memories lose roots--it's too preposterous to think that of you.

Our degree of purity determines what we remember so I suggest for joy you repent or whatever.

They try to draw me back in but no thanks I'm too sensitive to even hear what they're sayin'

You're the best at what you do and you know it. Stop looking around and just FOCUS: finish.

The modern herd has queenocidal tendencies: they want her to pay for being so queenly.

INNER CRITICS ARE OLD BASHERS

Recognize the inner critic--condemning voices--as mere implants of rascals in the past and rejoice.

Stand up and do what you're called to do or be degraded, disrespected and poo-pooed.

The best thing about eldering/retirement/sagacity is separation from dangerous youth of today.

The deliberately dumbed down have a quick fuse if you won't conform to their views, violence too.

Due to queenacide tendencies she must learn to hold her head up high/have high boundaries.

I don't care about what others are saying only what I'm saying so put your phones down/be sane.

It's important to realize your limitations. The first one is I can't take you, your chaos or friends.

DAFT LEFT

They pay experts to dig up dirt on you. They'll do anything to shut you up/ruin your rep too.

Alcoholics are charming social manipulators who endear themselves/side with authorities.

He was Jolly Jimmy to the world [the loving lunatic] but a mean monster to his wife he kept frantic.

Remember, they want you as the scapegoat--they need you in that position and that's it son.

HATRED OF SUPERIORITY: REGICIDE

Massive low self-esteem leads to the French Revolution: a mob beheading kings and queens.

The older fabulous female said: I have to finish my work not be derailed by a buncha soul tie hurts.

Dad repeated a million times: Hold Your Head Up High cuz he knew I was a queen/they'd say DIE.

Like all alcoholics Johnny's a charming social manipulator: yes sir, no sir, no ma'am, sorry.

What brings on the French Revolution mentality: trauma in an entire generation of ladies.

Feminism: the mother wasn't around or a bitch. About non-issues she'd get pissed, a total twit.

Jealousy is often subliminal--all they know is they hate you and such envy makes dangerous enemies.

It's the Dunning-Kruger effect of the dumb damning the smart, also known as homeostasis of stars.

FEMINISM IS A SEVERE UNDERTOW

DAFT LEFT

Despite feminism being "for women" it's a severe undertow to all she knows/she goes low.

I've made mistakes and gone against my beliefs but not you--you really believe all that, a dirty rat.

After things I say get so much dam flack I don't go back cuz why should I-- triggers hurt/sad sack.

It's crossing the Great Divide: miserable past to rosy future, sick systems to profitable/mature.

A bad leader is killed but a good one is overcome with joy/grateful he's no more ridiculed/annoyed.

The scary thing about narcissists is they always implode. It was all wind and fake you know.

LIMITLESS EVIL IN THE PEOPLE

I never knew people could get that bad. Like a bottomless pit, I was traumatized/felt dead.

"Can't trust nothin' but the love in your mother's eyes" and you sure can't trust that these days.

Narcissistic, toxic or immature people cannot be boundaried. They'll agree then bust it see.

A liberal is so mean he loves to get the public authorities on you, proudly with the sheriff on it too.

Any victim of a liberal gets a bit paranoid after facing their army of flying monkeys and authorities.

Here's the problem: people believe what they hear, that's what gives the gossiper power.

Heck of a thing when being good at something brings attack but that's this generation in fact.

DAFT LEFT

Don't worry cuz the worse/more outrageous you were then the more you're now a miracle man.

I spent years on the Potter's Wheel building back up. God has to debunk to reconstruct.

YOUR HOME IS YOUR KINGDOM

Let your home be your kingdom--nothing else out there matters. It's your center of gravity/pure.

In your kingdom you walk tall but if worrying over other's approval you feel [and are] painfully small.

Any pathbreaker may have voices yelling at him inside. That's from all those past resistances, aye.

Life is a solemn event. Yes there's rejoicing at times but things can suddenly turn so be vigilant.

The eccentric [loner] lives longer/looks younger cuz he doesn't have common social stressors.

Present purity wipes out the past--you gotta know that because if not you'll just repeat it/relapse.

We paid our dues and now want solitude. Total control, no surprises, each day God imbued.

DOUBLETHINK IS NEVER TRUE

All things cannot be true except liberals' DOUBLETHINK contradicting everything logical in you.

If you don't talk their NEWSPEAK which is constantly changing see you're outed, fired and a freak.

I was muted but got my voice back now. It was hell having no defense like a lamb before he's killed.

DAFT LEFT

You hear loud angry voices from the past--resistances to your messes or your talent and genius?

You're white, racist and a dirty rat. Get on your knees, pray for forgiveness and vote democrat.

Your mother walks up to you at age two with a gun--is it still her choice? Where does it end ok.

The wise relocate, the pretenders/sinners say "everything will be ok" and are taken/no escape.

You're white, racist and so are your kids. Kneel and vote democrat for total forgiveness.

WISE TO SUBTLE SABOTAGE

As you become more wise you're alert to subtle signs of sabotage. With great pros that's how it is.

People are callous cuz they adore Johnny: Alcoholics are so socially manipulative it isn't funny.

Amber Heard has no feminist support when it comes to the adoration of Hollywood scum like this.

Depp wanted to assassinate President Trump y'all--so instead he just raped Amber with a bottle.

Gaslighting: One drives another crazy by making her look like the sick one see.

The undertow is severe: most people fall into a pit unless they know how to fight against it.

Without Christ trauma swings many women into black magic: the occult, demon power of lunatics.

The best lesson you can give other people is to live your own life tho' they demand you be social.

DAFT LEFT

Even if I lose one proverb knowing it's gone forever I feel crazy: don't knock or call, see you later.

So you spent 50 years giving gift to the world it doesn't even want--so what, keep your chin up.

PSYCHOTIC TYRANTS IN HISTORY

The psychotics that get control of history want only worldwide dominance and patriots know this.

Most empires live 250 years, they implode from within then they have to fight for their freedom.

"Free speech is causing terror and must be banned". Doing/saying what you want is terrorism.

You must have SANCTIONED speech and only approved media is allowed on their platform see.

If we turn in guns and forget the second amendment they'll stop suing us in their courts, promised.

Homeland security's main job is to shut up the American people. Wow, this tyranny is so evil.

Those liberal champions of tolerance of yesterday are now the champs of intolerance today.

IT'S HOW THE SYSTEM DIVIDES THINGS

It's how the system is dividing things, no need to make sense. White supremacy is terror, that's it.

Any words you write DHS doesn't approve of it terrorism and it doesn't have to make sense son.

Those who advocate free speech are now "domestic threat actors" meaning prison for years.

DAFT LEFT

Free speech is now a terror threat. We're like most countries where you criticize, you're dead.

"These threat actors seek to exacerbate societal friction"--ever accusing us of what they're doin'

Wokers believe that when a crime is committed it's not the criminal's fault it's society and you all.

The ruling democrats think prisons and arrests just make things worse and law/order is a curse.

1920's Germans were into fashion, looking chic, style and narcissistic debauchery--then war see.

Black jazz musicians were a threat to German culture and society so they too faced treachery.

SYSTEMS OF CONSTANT TERROR

Any words you write DHS doesn't approve of is terrorism and it doesn't have to make sense son.

Biden's crack pipe handout: we've entered the insane final chapter of the total collapse of a regime.

People have hate and they focus it on groups they're allowed to since they're easy to attack.

I couldn't stand her: a phony haughty commie bitch and I don't care if she's my sister. Abuse Survivor

Narcissists will NEVER accept boundaries. You gotta give up your office hours idea honey.

I'm never bored or lonely but he can't get along without me so I just adapt being a nice lil' lady.

Sisters had hate in their heart and mom gave em the target: the youngest marked for success.

DAFT LEFT

HATRED AND ENVY IS HUMAN SOCIETY

Hatred and envy: I've had enough of this honey, I'm in retirement from the human social lunacy.

We're born in sin and that means hatred and jealousy as the default setting. Must be born again.

Satan's main markers are hatred and envy/jealousy. It hurt so much when they'd come at me.

Europe's Jews always wanted to believe the best but the switch from love to hate happened fast.

The mental tyranny and censorship is mind boggling, banning just cuz they don't like something.

All classes are mean when they have an accepted target for their hate but the lower do degrade.

LIVING WITH THE DUMBED

Living with dumb people you get good at fooling them just so they won't attack from boredom.

Of course I lied there was no other way to adapt and survive. They were suspicious/hostile, aye.

Of course I lied and I was good at it. I applied all intelligence to surviving with those lunatics.

All the crap I had to endure getting my Ph.D. in the Streets, who'd wanna be young again see.

I learned about interactional styles academically but not til I experienced em did I see the insanity.

It's a human jungle: female styles called "social". Lord, how come I was always the odd girl?

DAFT LEFT

Living in the jungle of mixed signals and weak egos I lived in terror like the jews years ago.

Even the great genius Beethoven was attacked by the town's children: that's how it happens son.

The youth accept pugnacity and even laugh at it. This means violence against the persecuted.

I lived in terror of older sisters who reminded me of Nazi concentration camp guards, hung later.

Narcissistic tyrants will ruin all your relationships even gossiping around on the day of your marriage.

They had hurt me so much out squeezed divine nectar called genius and a creative act, alas.

HOW TO MAKE GOLD

The extreme hurt from persecution pierced the mystic center and I made gold, an alchemal winner.

One can make gold on any issue. When you boil with frustration but don't give in = new you.

Usually one gives into the coping mechanism but when you don't, you make gold on the problem.

Once the big boil starts but you give into the addiction you must start the process all over again.

Having sealed the cauldron so none escapes, held in emotions explode to the horizon/you're ok.

You boil over, you give in to the addiction. The day you don't, now we're talkin' and life is rockin'.

It's hard surviving the bad mother archetype introjected [swallowed whole] but you can you know.

DAFT LEFT

Sign of a bad mother archetype: you feel homesick all the time and crave drugs to block it, aye.

How to survive missing father archetype: don't give into men as your fix, find yourself instead miss.

LESSONS LEARNED WHEN YOUNG

I could only get my Ph.D. in the Streets when young, able to endure the hard and painful lessons.

And now God willing I'm safe behind a gate in a life of beauty and learning without you interrupting.

Your vicious smear campaigns took terrible effect but in the long run I'm much stronger as the elect.

Life is a ladder and a budget. You were down now you're up, your time was controlled now not.

Don't let em control your time. Time is money, time is destiny, God designs the moment/it's divine.

I couldn't stand him coming over because he destroyed all my freedom to be alone and so clever.

I'd play music and he'd wanna talk thru it. He was in the left brain obviously and I'm done with it.

SOUL TIES ARE NOT LOVE

It may not be love but a soul tie. This is a sexual demon and obsessive lie, you don't need that guy.

That's all I gotta say, I'm so happy today having learned the lessons of life as I have portrayed.

My parents are eternally grateful that from my good example they found God while here still.

DAFT LEFT

Don't worry over painful past repeats. That was then--the hedge was down--but this is now.

Major recap: People come and go you know but God is eternal promising prosperity to the humble.

When ensnared all you think about is food, drugs, alcohol, sex. Temporal pleasures are a dam hex.

I wanted eternal pleasures and learned it in a fast. I learned about the moment, miracles at last.

I was ensnared by lower pleasures and was a monster not a treasure and I'm truly sorry sisters.

My favorite youtube psychiatrist showed disdain for Donald Trump and I unsubbed: bye chump!

Lord's friend: It's a miracle I'm living [survival driven] or didn't get locked up [God was overseeiin'].

PREJUDICE IS PROGRESSIVE

Nazism was progressive: first registered Jews, then anyone looking Jewish then anyone different.

Cultures have different threshold levels to novelty response. It's ANY old difference to some.

Feeling like a Jew in Nazi Germany is a false unfair comparison perhaps but true ol' chaps.

Hate is hate and it's hard to deal with it mate, and jealousy comes off that way. I drank/ate.

Is it any wonder I escaped to the desert wilderness, away from human society tension/stress?

When the dust settled the True Self was standing there, clean/crisp, a young eagle without compare.

DAFT LEFT

For people are cruel with hatred in them. Find key to live in this world/not get sick in bedlam.

BASHED STEREOTYPES

I thought youth were innocent, naive and eager to learn but I learned my lessons about moderns.

I thought old were nice and benevolent but learned my lessons about sadistic/lecherous old men.

Wisdom is knowing man has two sides. No one is good Jesus said—no, not ONE so don't confide.

Trust no man, put your trust in the Lord and life will turn out beautifully in the end in due course.

Behavior is always in context. Where disrespect they hate the bitch, with honor you're the best.

They screwed me on the will but God put holes in their bucket and doubled my accomplishments.

Recap: If you're a good girl or boy God rewards you but if not He can be the worst disciplinarian too.

Life starts good then you'll go thru rough spots. Never get complacent, be vigilant, rely on God.

Look at Europe's Jews in the thirties. They never thought that could happen but it did see.

Bible says "they think their houses will last forever". Watch complacency and always be prepared.

In this dire atmosphere of Biden disaster/world disrespect anything could happen, heck.

MALICIOUS PEOPLE DON'T CHANGE

DAFT LEFT

Don't bow down to malicious toxic people begging them to change. You won't and they won't ok?

Having frequent shallow exploitative parasitic relationships marks the psychopathic narcissist.

Continue in the ring of such mistreatment or go grey rock which is the least amount of contact.

Rise up and be the wonderful Christian soul God designed you to be, finally free of envy.

Go no-contact and now they'll just control how OTHERS see you and this for me was worst of all.

They deliberately cause family division/strife. A haughty spirit and wicked agenda for harm, aye.

They're lukewarm Christians--a teeny bit Christlike--with one foot in the world/one in heaven.

As Christians they sit on the fence. Tho' Sundays they go to church they're gossiping of course.

LUKEWARM CHRISTIAN SIBLINGS

Toxic Christian siblings are neither hot nor cold so God said "I will spit you out of My mouth".

As they dismantle their faith they fall astray and when weighed down by envy gone is their destiny.

Toxic Christian siblings live in denial--it's their go-to tactic we're all familiar with and God forbids.

Everything revolves around deception. They don't walk in truth and don't want you to either man.

If you are a whistle blower or truth seeker they will despise and lash out at you, it's the devil.

DAFT LEFT

You cannot change toxic siblings so the best can do is release them: Adios amigos, blessings. START

Not everyone is ready to walk away from all they've known in this journey. Choose season of joy.

There are **SEASONS**: of joy, crying, feasting, fasting, staying away, rejoining and eliminating.

If they're not your friends then they're your enemy. There is no lukewarm with God nor with me.

GO GREY ROCK

Don't stay silent to keep em comfortable, they'll call you stilted and dry as stone, be done that's all.

Grey rock means you stay at lowest contact as is possible. Don't respond anymore that's all.

During our grey rock we take a step back and reflect, we get clarity and can really see the craziness.

No contact: For once and for all, from this point on, we will not be communicating and that's that.

No more bowing down to demonic wishes, fearful antics, silent secrets, we're done with witches.

Liberation, healing and empowerment are coming your way now they're outa the way/your brain.

Not once did any one own up their harmful intentions so I have released them to God's hands.

To all **TIED** to toxic abusive family members God weeps for the brokenhearted/seeks to restore us.

Your True Self has been eclipsed by other people hating on you, for decades that's all you knew.

DAFT LEFT

EDUCATE GIRLS ON PSYCHOPATHS

As I look back what bothers me are the narrow escapes cuz I was so naive about psychopaths.

Girls: A psychopath will dispose of you if you get in their way and think nothing of it ok?

They will silently plan how to dispose of you and you won't know a thing. Believe this.

A sociopath is dangerous cuz he swam in muddy waters--he gets it from the gang etcetera.

A psychopath is dangerous cuz he's mean/doesn't care about a thing. No conscience, nothing.

To the psychopath the world is an instrument to fulfill his desires as he easily discards partners.

The three things that motivate a psychopath are profit, power or pleasure. Proceed with caution.

As we move from narcissism to psychopathy it's far more menacing, malevolent and exploitative.

TERRIFYING RELATIONSHIPS

These are terrifying relationships for the people in them. Walking on eggs is a severe understatement.

For those in psychopathic relationships, you are living with a terrifying stranger--hurry, EXIT it.

I never knew what he'd do next but I definitely knew SOMETHING was gonna happen, heck...

Psychopathy is a cunning element, praying on the weak and not wasting much time lovebombing.

DAFT LEFT

I was perfect then deranged from the influence of other people like those described above.

Scared me half to death, suddenly realizing I'd moved in with a monster after burning my bridges.

I was sick with fear of this man, a primal panic felt deep in the stomach called the Solar Plexus.

SICK WITH FEAR AND PANIC

It was the same sick with fear panic felt in the gut when betrayed by my sister and family thugs.

This was when I was young and foolish/didn't know what I was doing, and I'd be helping.

I didn't know what people were like until then. I had been sheltered in a conservative home.

A bottomless pit of evil, a deep cavern, monsters of the devil, abusers and users of all that's good.

Your living situation changes quickly with a psychopath. They move right in and take over fast.

Does whatever the hell he wants. Don't get in his way or you're toast, he's basically an adolescent.

They sniff out the vulnerabilities in a potential target and exploit them cuz they're good at it.

They set honey traps/exploit fears to get leverage which they do immediately, it's their whole thing.

DARK AND MENACING PRESENCE

You're in the presence of something dark and menacing and that's why you can't sleep darling.

DAFT LEFT

Psychopathic relationships use fear and terror and thus the recovery is more complicated by far.

He hurt me so much/I was so scared of this monster I got a disorder and stopped eating altogether.

This was when I was young and strong enough to endure these things in order to learn of earthlings.

They are cruel/think nothing of it. Most goes under the radar/is forgotten completely, deleted.

I know what it's like as a child/wife of an alcoholic and what one can expect from psychopathics.

Thank you God for all these lessons, my Ph.D. in the streets, that took a season of endurance.

Serial relationships shows you are one of many targets. It's how he subsists cuz he's so good at it.

CULTURE TEACHES MENTAL ILLNESS

Culture teaches mental illness and what is SEEN as mental illness in any era in any place on earth.

It was frightening living in a small desert town where the Dunning-Kruger effect was in control.

It taught me more than a library of books living with Dunning Krugers tho' it was a bummer.

You had a demon in you honey so the particulars aren't important/should be forgotten immediately.

Stop this crap worrying about the past and realize it was a demon and you were too dam weak at first.

All the particulars of how you screwed up aren't important tho' I'm sure they were numerous.

DAFT LEFT

Your enemies from a past perished while you have thrived. Or lost their teeth if they didn't die.

TOXIC SHAME PASSED DOWN

It helps to know your toxic shame is passed down, not from something you've done tho' you have hon'.

From his deathbed dad was ashamed of youthful sins. It's all he talked about: passed-down shame.

I remember an angry woman vociferating with her mouth as big as a cavern--a bottomless pit.

Any society which robs Peter to pay Paul can always count on Paul's vote. Dinesh D'Souza

It's authoritarianism cloaked as moral righteousness and that's the ambience on all college campuses.

Don't watch mainstream news, it's all bull. Store food/ water/ammo and stay inside until it's all done.

Arrogance brings itself down through overreach. Isn't it funny how they do themselves in always.

The ego says "I look good all the time no matter what I do" because it can't face it's not in control too.

That's how the ego brings the narcissist down: in denial he goes about like he still wears the crown.

The narcissist can't see his variations depending on his behavior, he thinks he's always the same sir.

Writers are everything. Both Golden Girls and Raymond had lousy shows when writers were varying.

Being single is like being thrown to the wolves. The evil tsunami flows in/you'd better have defense.

DAFT LEFT

Liberals instantly know each other, a silent club of superiority--a dyad of locked collusion see.

Feminists unwisely think they can be independent. In this world? Are they insane? You need a mate.

SILENT CLUB OF SUPERIORITY

Find a mate and make HIM love you then he'll handle all the others--it is so efficient this way, it's of God.

Feminists don't wanna make a man love them, they think they shouldn't have to work for anything.

Without a man as my fence that means i gotta face a world that's dense and the outcome's bad/by chance.

They were violent towards me in '87 so of course it's extreme now since each generations worse.

A world where Dunning-Kruger's in effect: the dumb are over the smart though they're a defect.

I can hear people yelling at me, do I need a lobotomy? It's constant frenzy/usually from women/frenemies.

With so much pot and good music how can we go wrong? We need a good home and don't forget God.

Affluent libs are all for socialism until the gov wants to move a couple families into their big home.

I guess from being a triple Pisces when I went wrong it was triple wrong and very weird of the underworld.

But then when I repented all that energy went to creative good and it was thrice as good/well understood.

Many decades were insane, in a fog, an empty shell but wounded as hell. As denial lifts I can recall.

DAFT LEFT

MOST WRONG BECOMES MOST RIGHT

Find a mate, then work it all out together. Not "social" and independent while your best years vapor.

A writer writes and it's not for the money. It's as natural as a bird singing, in all fields that's the way.

He was so imposing in those days but that's before he had his wings clipped by life in this day and age.

Being a conservative is about independence. You have no freedom as a liberal, you conform in a dance.

They need to be programmed into individualism, entrepreneurism, patriotism, limited government.

A personality style is different from a disorder even if it is grandiose, narcissistic, entitled, unempathic.

When reality is too harmful, painful, traumatic and unacceptable as it is, defense mechanisms kick in.

So as to ameliorate anxiety and regulate the internal environment like moods in order to survive.

The mechanisms adapt by changing reality: splitting, seeing it differently, relating only to good, etc.

It's either change reality or disintegrate. It's so harsh and impossible to accept you see it as great.

Imagine democrat disaster from: MORE foreign workers/population growth and LESS enforcement.

Arrests being made day/night all over the world and Biden's going to prison/Trump'll be in again.

ARCHETYPES POSITIVE AND NEGATIVE

DAFT LEFT

I've lived thru all of the archetypes I mention and having one foot in the coffin it's really embarrassin'.

Queen Bee and Jezebel are archetypes or grooves we fall into when at that level: caricatures of humans.

He was dashing and distinguished at 16 but when I saw him again at 60 he looked like a cartoon freak.

Many decades were insane, in a fog, an empty shell but wounded as hell. As denial lifts we see it all.

We should have seen it coming sirs, the progressive's unprincipled, menacing, incendiary purge.

One is grandiose, feels superior and thin-skinned but still it's just a style not a mental illness with him.

How it started [fear]: Writing was a desperate attempt to be heard so they would know I was here.

When your hedges are down cuz trauma dissolved em then life is pure hell, invaded by all of THEM.

Another thing trauma dissolves is morals. Now you're not just a beggar but a slut, that's how it goes.

What is a slut? It's an unpaid whore cuz doing your ex a favor is low but familiar--need God for sure.

With boundaries every minute's my own, alone. Without em the evil world flows in--there's no hope.

You have to tell your story or else someone else will tell it for you in a way you may not like.

To liberals, unity means the absence of opposition. There is no compromise just destroying reputation.

REAL MEN ARE CONSERVATIVE

DAFT LEFT

Politicizing the justice system is beginning of the end. Conservatives get punished, liberals don't friend.

Inciting violence, chemical warfare, domestic terrorism: labels designating punishments we should fear.

Silencing and cancel culture is the left but conservatives are the champions of free speech/intellect.

It's not that women are bad, they're just trusting. That's why with foreign invasion they kill all the men.

It's women who are serving the beast. They suckup to government like it's daddy or the priest.

The real men are always conservative. They don't do wild things jeopardizing a family/home they love.

Dumbing people down so you can hurt and control them: that's the real reason we shouldn't trust em.

Tearing a former president apart cuz he wasn't a globalist—to scare any other populist leaders out of it.

It's a global consortium of corps who hate free market but want fascist monopoly to carry out eugenics.

I surmised: Joe Biden runs an international crime family against our nation and is fully compromised.

WIFEY: Because you couldn't think that deeply you labeled your husband as crazy but he was right, see?

POLITICS SPLITS THE HICKS

Because of your husband's conservative political views the state decreed mandatory drugging all cuza you.

The brain is split. Jack Dorsey listens to Alex Jones but to the extreme left he couldn't get farther out.

DAFT LEFT

PTSD is like being in a war where there's never any R & R. It can go on for decades as body wears out.

I'm atypical of women my age. I'm enjoying that rare distinction nowadays tho' it's only temporary.

I'm atypical of women my age. Though it's only temporary I'm enjoying that rare distinction nowadays.

The WAR was for my identity, which meant everything after early trauma of a broken bond/disconfirming.

The sick family system is an Identity Struggle. We identify ourselves against the background of others, yuk!

How my sister saw me terrified me. I'd do anything to prove that image wrong, so it propelled me.

IDENTITY STRUGGLES AND BOOZE

If I dare drank to deal with the sadness of identity disconfirmation it was TOTAL ID ruination.

They'd trigger me to drink like the white man and the Indian with a genetic proclivity towards alcoholism.

And so I turned to pot and food. The food ruined body, ended on juices; the pot adjusted my moods.

The reality I was forced to accept was insane. I needed an attitude adjustment not a crutch like alcoholism.

They wanted me drunk to control me. That was the last straw between alcohol and me, 30 yrs free.

It's a genetic proclivity/potential. Ancestor said: our clan ends in the gutter or speaks from the pulpit.

They liked it when I got drunk and went crazy like a wild-woman from all their contradictions!

DAFT LEFT

That's what made me stop. Not the unbearable hangovers but being controlled by dumb idiots on top.

On unbearable hangovers: The last time I drank 30 years ago I ended up in ER and went baseline sir.

EVIL RISES UP THEN SO DOES GOOD

As evil rises good is rising as well. We can't forget that in the face of this irrational and illogical hell.

It's a totally female-centric legal system--she takes him to the cleaners and the courts are all behind her.

The Creative Act is a literal structure in nature. When complete it attracts pollination/a producer.

The female desire for free stuff and to be taken care of: that's one reason they suckup to daddy gov.

Main thing is: don't be surprised. That's what they do--they're doing what they do, compromised.

You dare to speak a narrative they disagree with and they'll go to any length to silence you quick.

Here he didn't even have a right to talk to you but he became your master and you his slave girl.

They are smug, self-righteous neoliberal fascists. Don't fret just expect/learn how to deal with this.

THE DAFT, DAFT LEFT

While we slept they wove their webs but the sun always comes back and the heat is felt by celebs.

This whole thing shows how low these demons are, and the fact elites love and adore them as stars.

DAFT LEFT

It's no accident Nemesis will wipe out both coasts, that's where the filthy liberals live and boast.

Drip, drip, drip: a gradual thing but the liberals are so dumb they couldn't see it happening.

This has been the reign of the pedophile devil worshippers, in elites (men/women) way up there.

Harrison Ford looked out disgusted at the Oscar audience clapping wildly for the pervert notorious.

Celebrating a Hollywood child rapist who's a fugitive from justice.

They have collapsed, they know they're the past. But like Hillary they don't go away/keep us the sass.

When asked to go see a movie the kids said "can't we stay home and play cards?" It's over, you see?

SEXUALIZE AND BRAIN DAMAGE KIDS

Sexualize your children, brain damage em, inject em and even CNN admits it lowers IQ 20 points, friends.

The democrats, republicans, media, academia and Hollywood all hate Trump and you mimic it bud.

Where was your leftist anti-war rage when Obama was bombing seven countries simultaneously?

Criticizing a black president just didn't make commercial sense.

Eminem you're not edgy or counterculture but a 44 year old has-been and an anti-Trump poll chaser.

He's a flop so joins the fake anti-Trump resistance by conforming to boring virtue-signaling.

He made his name ridiculing mindless dull pop culture but now has become mediocre, a bore.

DAFT LEFT

BRAINLESS VIRTUE SIGNALING

They don't know anything they're just virtue signaling and getting attention from the peanut gallery.

Liberals always use anecdotes to disprove you: so-and-so did this, so-and-so was a victim: dismiss.

The dumbed down condition of America never been so evident as now, bashing our president.

Liberal culture can't debate only blow whistles, swear, flip the bird or other gross/childish gestures.

They teach em **WHAT NOT HOW** to think and thus they become mindless robots repeating this stink.

Stand against brainwash by liberal teachers. They've no right to destroy minds and some are lechers.

HOLLYWOOD IS CORRUPT

Hollywood is corrupt. The strong prey upon the weak and no one (until now) is brought to account.

They love humanity but mistreat people--it's always the abstract with evil.

They love Obama cuza the sleek superficials while ignoring what's under: death and destruction.

Unrepentant hypocrite Kaepernick defends Castro: sick!

Eminem is no longer authentic, daring or counter culture but a washed up whiny middle aged millionaire.

How dense could he be thinking a cute starlet'd wanna watch a diseased hippo rub on himself on a tree?

Congratulations, all starlets on screen no longer need pretend attraction to Harvey Weinstein.

DAFT LEFT

The devil isn't a trailblazer, he's a swindler that leaves you starving to death in the desert.

Had to sleep with Harvey to be in movies.

UGLINESS FROM LEFTIST DESIGNERS

Ugliness coming from leftist designers: Men Who Hate Women Clothes Design: Yuk three times

Creation is an act of resistance.

His fashion show was called Dirt and it was.

I am Eminem, I am enlightened. I don't have an argument but sure do hope that you're frightened.

I am the great Eminem, I have a potty mouth, I am rebellious! I'm filthy rich, see my black power fist!

Just democrat talking points, rage on a stick. Don't know a thing but listen to me cuz I'm rich! SICK

It's frightening when there is no justice--living in a society who can't see right/wrong or distinguish.

Drew a line in the sand, for or against. That's ok Eminem cuz now we all hate your washed-up guts.

Americans are sick of racist and anti-Trump rhetoric posing as entertainment.

Trump is the golden touch (3 trillion so far) but scum like Eminem are trying to start a race war.

We're sick of Eminem types using public platforms to trash our president. Retire, bro--your demise is imminent.

Eminem's unhinged Trump attack only strengthened us--the Streisand Effect made us bigger as such.

DAFT LEFT

Eminem hopped on the wrong train--should have learned from Kaperneck the country's sick of this drain.

HOLLYWOOD SCUM ATTACKS TRUMP

At Eminem's rant tempers flared. Why attack Trump in every performance? We're bored and angered.

They hate Trump cuz they want his power but will never get it since it's Satan vs. Man of the Hour

Rich rapper Eminem resents Trumps power over him so disguises outrage to his career advantage.

The washed up aging rap star Eminem unveiled his disgusting song to the BET liberal black throng.

As much as celebs hate Trump they make a mint from slandering him. It's the style with Hollywood scum.

Eminem's lyrics declare war on those disliking kaperneck so we hate both your guts, you and that wreck.

The new NFL anthem says F-you to anyone supporting Trump. We love watching you self-destruct!

Eminem's line in the sand deleted us who want entertainment, not preached to bashing our president.

Rappers and racist athletes didn't draw the line, we rejected the swine.

Eminem we used to love your inputs but now we hate your guts.

Creeps like Eminem hate flicks that don't push a divisive message. They're all like that, the dregs.

If we killed the NFL we can kill rap (won't sell)

We all have to start somewhere and you're waking up fast--it'll be glorious!

Not only does aging Eminem need Civics he needs a kick in the pants.

DAFT LEFT

You're either for our country and ACTUAL unity, or on the losing end of a tired talking point, truly.

HANKERING FOR THE DEAD PAST

You're hankering for the past, but not for them--they've lost God's spirit, they have no significance.

No amount of rhetoric elitist entertainers spew about our president will stop him from MAG@again.

What Eminem is really mad about is Trump kept his promise but that's why we love him, our president.

They don't have the intellectual maturity to think for for themselves so hop on Eminem's train to hell.

Eminem should join the Harvey cesspool--we know it's all the same bag anyway: the very uncool.

Of course the media is hailing it as brave. That's always the way but it's Eminem who misbehaves.

Eminem: can't wait for fake news line-by-line analysis as they all nod in agreement about our president.

Eminem's now a politically relevant misogynist. And loony left loves the contradiction (still can't see it).

This peer-approved rap shows us who they all are--mere pap--and will go by the wayside as crap.

So angry that a white man could be superior to a black elitist. Really, in this day/age you're that racist?

An aging, frumpy, irrelevant white rapper acting like he's black and we're all laughing at this sad sack.

It's easy to recall predictable lines from this noise: it's all pat, trite, echoed talking points of little boys.

DAFT LEFT

GET BUSY AND DO YOUR THING

A painter paints. A writer writes. A cook cooks and a builder builds so why are you watching TV, Bill?

We can't stop this fist revolution cuz for four decades we've been dumbed down preparing for doom.

I'm just happy Eminem has moved from threatening his mother or wife. Greg Gutfeld

Eminems "rap" was so boring. Not a single line is a surprise, he's lost all originality just mindless warring.

Was he really "ground breaking"? NO Eminem's a tired old loser using Trump for moneymaking.

Trump's "locker talk" meant nothing but Hollywood covered for sex abuser Harvey--how contradictory.

They hate President Trump but ignore PIG Weinstein's sexual predation--can you even imagine?

Hollywood hypocrisy will destroy their history.

The left isn't funny anymore. Comics are mean spirited so go ahead, make us hate it/we want no more!

They bash Trump for a mere conversation alone, but cover up for a fat pig pervert to keep his throne.

Harvey gave 700 grand to dems, none to reps--funneled to Hollywood, of course they're blind/deaf.

It's not both sides cuz media's quite for the left (Hollywood $ goes left) but never shut up re: Trump.

HOLLYWOOD IS EXTENSION OF DEMS

Hollywood: extension of democratic party

DAFT LEFT

FOX is 50% against Trump.

No matter what they do the left always portrays themselves as the victims. Even ol' Harvey the scum.

They're not a "bubble within a bubble", you need a purge pail to watch awards: trouble not subtle.

Spewing about politics when they don't know a lick and blocking the other side with a swift kick.

You can't have a opinion other than the socialist mindset or you don't get a job in Hollywood I'll bet.

Clinton, Harvey, Weiner: the party for women is not the left, that's a no-brainer.

Conservatives believe women should be honored/held in favor--compare that to Harvey or Weiner.

Mainstream America knows there's a double standard but we still have the guns and votes fellas.

WHO sends his own daughter to work for a sexual predator? The greatest predator himself, Obama.

For 30 years Weinstein was praised by Hollywood and democrats. Even when they knew, the rats.

Left calls us insubstantial, frivolous, trollish or clownish to justify not rationally debating with us.

If lucky enough to be American, Australian, English or Canadian you'll have free speech and capitalism.

Human rights and capitalism made the west the greatest in the history of our species. Milo Yiannopolus

Men don't just matter--they are essential. For 100 years boy scouts turned boys into men, influential.

BLATANT HYPOCRASY OF MEDIA NEWS

DAFT LEFT

CNN has interviewed mass-murdering dictators but draws the line with Milo, that's the way it goes.

Liberals hate the boy scouts (cuz they're wholesome, non-ironic, patriotic) so they seek to deconstruct.

He's no rap god he's a demon from hell.

More sex hex from the left: Ben Affleck

Eminem's a failed puppet of globalists/everyone (in real world) hates him now--keep digging that hole!

NFL/failed rappers: Keep losing, we love it. Meanwhile we'll be winning cuz we're so far above it.

Eminem's talking points heard a 1000 x from dems yet this is the "best political writing of the year?"

Reading off teleprompters trying to act cutting edge.

Americans hate posers and love individualism. It's the spirit of overcoming elitism (Eminem) for freedom.

Eminems are trying to turn us against each other and hate our country so we can be conquered.

We recognize globalist mercenaries trying to pimp us out like that little bitch Eminem. Alex Jones

Eminem isn't a real man who would take on the globalists like a Donald Trump.

The pro-American/military thing at the end was just to sucker you. Eminem hates it all/Americans too.

Eminem is a traitor who hates America and is a dirty little coward who play-acts like a black thug.

HOLLYWOOD FAKE THUGS: EMINEM

DAFT LEFT

Eminem's a little coward owned by people like Weinstein. Alex Jones

Here all these disasters are happening to unite us and this fake black thug Eminem whines to divide us.

Just another fake gangster thug posing as if political reading off a teleprompter doing a terrible job.

CNN: Eminem was "greatest performance they saw in their lives"--how hollow, desperate, snide.

We crossed your line in the sand you little wanna-be thug Eminem.

Mr. Satanic illuminati jihadi fake thug: silly

Holier than thou virtue signaling about bigotry/racism yet his songs are about killing women, hmm.

Eminem's lyrics are about murdering and raping women regularly.

There is a line in the sand and Eminem stands with rich celebrities, elitists, globalists: UnAmerican.

All the kings men couldn't put Eminem back together again: another failed loser trying to stay relevant.

He poses like tough guy growing up hard in streets of Detroit--but he's the creation of MTV, kid you not.

They called it "fierce" we call it "fake"

Wow we're really cutting edge, Eminem doesn't like Trump!

Keep it up: NFL threatening to take a knee again. You've already lost half your audience--don't stop!

God vs. devil: always remember who's stronger.

Tho' liberal celebs fawn over Eminem's freestyle Trump takedown, learn the truth/spread it around.

DAFT LEFT

FREEDOM IS SEXIEST

We are the sexiest thing, real freedom, true renaissance (so they come here) and Eminem hates it!

In one mindless video Eminem has destroyed his career irrevocably cuz deplorables are the majority.

You put yourself in the man's world of politics now expect the whirlwind cuz it's gonna be rough, man.

Eminem fall down. Eminem dumb dumb. Punk Ass Eminem. Alex Jones

The reactions are so illuminating: "Eminem's the best political writing of the year". Keith Olbermann

In the 50's people weren't obvious sinners (decency prevailed) but now they are (liberalism failed).

The point about Harvey is not him, but all those who covered for him over 30 years with a million women.

Hollywood scum who covered for Harvey also came against the victims.

IN HOLLYWOOD RAPE IS OK IF IT'S GAY

Men assaulted by men in Hollywood--couldn't say anything or be called homophobic by gay mafia.

Don't say "gay" say what it is: homosexual. We're sick of being told what words are acceptable.

SICK: Hollywood is where the gay mafia is thick and you don't confront or you're up a creek/tricked.

Left sees moral equivalence between Harvey's antics and Trump--walk away when hearing this crap.

Gay rape in military up 15-fold since came outa closet. It's explosive when don't care who knows it.

DAFT LEFT

Men ashamed to admit they're raped: It's ok cuz it's gay.

Men getting raped is ok. Our men are tough, won't say anything about it cuz it's just "gay".

It's like a handshake--men grabbing men even in meetings. A deep rabbit hole and hard to believe.

Not called "assault" but a handshake ritual of dominance. It's common with men esp. the prominent.

EMMYS ARE A BASH-TRUMPFEST

The three hour Emmys were a bash-Trumpfest, second lowest ratings of all time cuz we're sick of this.

Women's Health is another word for abortion.

Lady said "I see now why I went to work in my pajamas--it was the anti-depressants", that explains it.

Hollywood is boring, their movies are formulaic.

Knowingly exposing people to HIV no longer illegal in Calif: penalty is no more than a parking ticket.

Brown's a Satanist cuz that's what they do: kill multitudes with diseased blood/other ways too.

California wants communists to hold state jobs.

Drain the swamp, save the republic!

It's easy to take freedom from people if they don't know what freedoms are-- like rights of the unborn.

The bible is from the One True God not "little gods". India has 300,000 little gods--that is paganism.

We will not rest until the burden of Obamacare is off the backs of American citizens. Mark Walker (R-NC)

DAFT LEFT

We're returning moral clarity to our view of the world and the many challenges we face. Donald Trump

God used the flawed. He used sinner Kings to accomplish great things: I hear Trump and am awed.

Separation of Church and State was there to protect churches from government, not the opposite!

California: warmth and beauty but what about the policies?

RINOS AND NEOCONS JUST AS BAD

RINOS and NeoCons: Old establishment folks reading off teleprompters trying to act cutting edge.

The American experiment was not the "state" but the absence of the state-- the smallest gov possible.

Standing for the flag is not agreeing with the state but the American experiment which is no-state.

Leftists don't want Americana (less gov) but MORE gov--socialism and tyranny: this is noteworthy.

Young males. That's what's invading and destroying the whole world and even now few go to jail.

Lord calls it an abomination and I believe Him.

Hillary's a feminist but never showed the slightest interest in the abuse of women in Islam, honest.

We stand with heroes not a bunch of rich, entitled, arrogant, ungrateful anti-American degenerates.

Trump asks Chicago leaders why so many murders? But liberal management won't ever answer.

As Trumpsters we don't make a loud stink like the others but we're out there/we really matter.

DAFT LEFT

The Chicago cop said "if they'd unleash us this would be over immediately" but liberals say NO WAY.

DEMOCRATS RUINED CITIES FOR 100 YEARS

Democrats have ruled inner cities for 100 years and that's why they're devastated/so many murders.

The anti-Trump thing is not good for your bottom line or your brand--decent folk love him, he's our man.

Because radicalism has been allowed to go unchecked for so long, it's gone full circle as it implodes.

Children are learning in school that America is evil. That's the exact opposite to what is true, people.

Anyone who resembles the founders of this country is stained with blood guilt and should be punished?

They see our entire past as a movie of bigotry and oppression, seeing racism everywhere and we're one.

We respect our flag not cuz we worship the state but we love small government/WE decide our fate.

Girl wants to be a star, goes to Hollywood and immediately taken over, and now they're raping America.

Turn away from debates with liberals. We need to conserve our energy not fight those going to hell.

I don't care how impressed you are with a liberal, don't argue. I'm telling you: it'll be the end of you.

Many great artists/musicians are liberals. Don't argue no matter what their impressive credentials!

A great painter should just paint not talk about liberal politics cuz a great scholar he clearly ain't.

DAFT LEFT

To make her clothing line she had to marry Harvey then bully other women to wear her clothes, really.

I find Milo appalling and always have. Ben Shapiro

LIBERAL PSYCHOLOGIST SCAM

Liberal psychologists' misdiagnosis of Trump just proves what they always say: they're all crazy.

We're not sending more blacks for prison time, they're going there in exact proportion to their crimes.

Being a provocateur just for the sake of violating taboos is worthless. Ben Shapiro

Feminists don't care about female genital mutilation, forced marriages or acid thrown in girl's faces.

They argue with idiotic narratives. Refuse em, tell em to save their boring communist parrotings.

Leftism is the perfect theory for glueing up the brain. Trotsky

Five men holding one down is not "consent" and it happens all the time. But then "anything gay is ok"

Love your home, do what you should. Don't argue, does no good--they lack education, hearts of wood.

Shut up, your opinion means nothing. You're a professional victim and for that you are just bluffing.

They aren't your opinions, but those of your gender studies professor. Shut your pie-hole, messer.

You're not retreads of the old hippies. They fought for free speech which you banned in the cities.

Savagery is the new leftist modernism. Can you appreciate these wonders of multiculturalism?

DAFT LEFT

Feminists were against Hugh Heffner but with time he's a hero "liberating us from constraints" ya know.

HEF EMPOWERED WOMEN TO BE VERMIN

in the 60's women saw Heffner as objectifying women but since then he "empowered us" to be vermin.

How did Heffner empower women if their men were looking at nude pictures of others besides them?

Men who respect women don't revel in porn but somehow Hugh became a cultural hero/a new norm.

How is vulgarization winning the culture war?

Hugh Heffner's entire ideology: When women age out of beauty, cast them aside like an old bitty.

Hugh Heffner's message to America: promiscuity is virtue. Feminists love him cuz they like that too.

Heffner: Did he help or destroy marriages? He was a pornographer so that is the answer isn't it.

"Repressive climate of the era" means: man was man, woman was woman and couples stayed together.

Men stopped relating to real women after being hypnotized by fantasy females in magazines, demons.

Thru psychotic shock from sick system you flushed it out--the original trauma--and could start again.

They celebrate Hugh's life as a civil rights activist rather than a publisher of pornography and nudists?

Hollywood is boring, their movies are formulaic. Americans are bored and voting with their dollar.

DAFT LEFT

Everything from Hollywood is so stale, unimaginative and tedious. Paul Joseph Watson

CULTURE IS INTRIGUE, WISDOM, BEAUTY

Culture should be intrigue, lust for knowledge, appreciation of beauty--not a obscene sewer of vacuity.

Goal of hideous art: undermine western civilization leaving us open to subversion and capitulation.

TV shows broken families, emasculated males figures, aberrant nihilistic youths amoral and insane.

Late stages of society: bizarre behavior proliferates and is legitimatized by the dominant culture.

Once we absorb the degeneracy our moral filter is irreparably damaged but it comes back with Jesus.

Even for active exercise nuts, the more TV you watch the more depressed you get--that's the stats.

Hypersexualization of culture normalizes cheating and betrayal cuz everyone else is doing it too.

Hypersexuality in pop culture leads to ruined relationships and failed marriages: miserable/lonely.

FAMOUS WITH NO TALENT

Being famous used to require having actual talent. Now you're just born for it or feel entitled to it.

They mimic what they see on TV and make asses of themselves as the culture slides down, see?

Now, the degree of fame is tantamount to degree of tasteless debauchery they inflict on the world.

DAFT LEFT

Vulgarity has replaced talent (as it debases it) and if you don't believe it just watch evil Hollywood.

The more vulgar and ostentatious the better. Compare that to class and elegance decades earlier.

Not fulfillment, meaning nor authenticity but Narcissism is the ultimate measure of importance in celebrity.

POPULAR CULTURE IS VULGAR

Popular culture is so invasively vulgar it's a factor in radicalization of islamic terror--goes together.

Our popular culture does NOT represent western civilization but a weapon to reassert cultural Marxism.

First they immerse themselves in the culture then bomb it as only means of repentance/that's now bad it is.

Since people are being killed for standing for Trump they bash him instead: they are the swamp.

You'll be accepted by those hearing with tickled ears but it'll send them to hell so you should fear.

Those who are left after these measures will live in austerity while they are untra rich and tax exempt.

Eminem got rich from music of gay slurs, domestic violence glorification and other filthy lyrics.

You --- and ---- are happily pushing Trump supporters away but you will regret that some day.

You put down Trump, you put down everyone who voted for him. Are we dumb? You must think so bud.

Anti-Trumpers like The View reject entire middle America. They only love their buds on coasts, yah.

DAFT LEFT

Now we'll see how far you fall when spitting in our faces for we are the majority with status.

Polarity is so wide once a Trumpster hears one tiny sign of your tendency to bash and he'll divide.

That desire to be edgy turned many from gentle Christianity to Islam which hiphop fit into, ma'am.

HIP HOP AND ISLAM IN YOUNG MEN

Hip Hop, Islam: Violence taken for granted as part of the matrix.

21st century war is an info-war and it's HERE on facebook and twitter.

You go up against the champion populist Donald Trump and you're career hits the wall or slumps.

You will be politically destroyed by going after Trump.

Lesson of Megyn Kelly: going with the establishment when it's crashing and burning is not a good idea.

Democrats fought for slavery during the Civil War.

TRUMP RESPECTS WOMEN

I've never seen a man more respectful to women than Donald Trump. James Robison

Was Obama respectful to women marrying a man and buying $65,000 worth of "hot dogs"? Come on...

Hating Trump brands em as know-nothing conformists to liberal gobbledygook. Good, ignore the kooks.

It's this generation calling themselves Christian then male stripping? Come on man this is filthy leaven.

Life's too serious to be acting that way anymore--we're blessed with Trump who saved us from horror.

DAFT LEFT

If you don't love and adore Donald Trump our wonderful president, kindly get off of my page.

I'm sick of arguing with you creeps. You want us under globalist tyranny but you're about to reap.

THE COASTS ARE EVIL DEM STRONGHOLDS

The coasts are largely evil, democrat strongholds. They feel superior and hate us deplorables.

We're not gonna forget. Tho' we must forgive that doesn't mean we gotta see your ugly face again.

I said to the silly liberal questioner just trying to rattle my cage: you're boring, go away.

Young males happily raping, killing and pillaging across the world. See it as young males/no other labels.

It's all young males: BLM, Antifa, Isis--can't you see this?

Gangs on the coasts are young males raping, murdering and pillaging in hyper-masculinity.

See it for what it is--young boys wanna do these things. It scratches an itch and is transforming.

This is what happens to young males without a father in most cases, combined with sick culture.

Older people wanna live their own life in privacy and freedom not protest supposed transgressions.

The progeny of broken families without fathers: boy gangsters closing in, it's all a strange karma.

Calling founders phony is just SJW made up stuff. These brilliant geniuses planned our freedom, bud.

DAFT LEFT

The driving out of God without the capacity to identify evil is the great tragedy of the 21st century.

When David Wolfe put down Trump he suddenly became crap to us.

DEPLORABLES ARE >HALF THE COUNTRY

Deplorables are more than half this country. You don't put down Trump unless you wanna fail quickly.

He's against Trump who saved us from danger! He hopped on the bandwagon, a false teacher.

Most child actors become losers--but was it not what they went thru with Hollywood's abusers?

He wrote "ex gays" and was fired, lost tenure, mysteriously died. You don't say it's a choice, guys.

It's a symptom of disease to see racism behind everything.

"There is no reasoning with bigots you can only crush them": that's how the left sees us friends.

Calling someone a "racist" is a conversation-ender, not a starter. Tucker Carlson

Everything the left doesn't like is "racist" so how can we talk anymore? We can't, move on/ignore.

White people have a right to exist and have pride in their identity--that is not "white supremacy".

Since we cannot change the past of slavery, white people are to be eternally and forever guilty?

Though it's a small minority doing it, black crime is ten times more than whites but we're to blame for it?

It's not a hate crime that whites exist and western Christian civilization was by far the best.

DAFT LEFT

Old men Snoop and Eminem dissing Trump for profit is so predictable of these fake thugs/nuts.

OLD RAPPERS NEED CIVICS

Old rappers will do anything to stay relevant like hop on the bandwagon but it sure isn't genius.

Highest marketing strategy is to diss Trump cuz that's what the brainwashed public bought.

With old rappers there is no excellence cuz they show their ignorance having never had Civics.

Eminem is a weak punk not like Trump who goes to war against globalist gangs and thugs.

Completely dissipated and out of creative ideas they gotta scrape the barrel with this sleaze.

THEY'RE CRUDE AND RUDE

They're crude/don't know right from wrong, saying wrong is right/hating good, inciting riots with song.

TV sitcoms create fantasies of whites killing others so now BLM targets whites with hammers.

The look so self-righteous as they create division and incite wars. These are globalist pawns: the stars.

Either they don't know any better or totally bought and paid for. There's no way, it's a no-brainer.

Globalists created the thug personality for MTV--any way to debase us and bring in immorality.

It's not what they did, it's why'd you fall in with such lower companions--that's the question hard to fig.

DAFT LEFT

People are so dumbed down it'd be easy to rile em up to a killing spree and they're well-funded ya see.

It's all a made-up thing, lies to create division. That's always how tyrants take control: snoopdoggin'.

THEY'RE PAID TO BRAINWASH US

They're paid to brainwash us with this stuff--via our senses/love of song--but we've had enough.

The elites are laughing at us--how easy it is to control the masses especially with dumbasses.

This influence is highly dangerous so mark my words don't argue/debate and life will be fabulous.

Crazy that Obama and Bush came out yesterday when they're both so loathed by the base.

Doesn't Bush/Obama get it that we've broken with them, that we hate them/see thru globalist vermin?

Where does Bush get off bashing Trump after his unjust wars? Lies, crimes, globalist whores.

They are discredited, despised and no one believes a word they say, disgusting sold out sleaze.

AMERICA'S COMING BACK

America's getting back to independence so when we see these sellouts it's like snakes or rodents.

They want you to think everyone's against us but it's not true--it's the loudest vs. God's crew.

I'm trying to flush you out if you hate Trump or love Obama. If you're that dumb get out not kiddin' ya.

DAFT LEFT

Bill Clinton's friend Epstein supplied underage girls to Weinstein: the elite liberals are fiends.

Weinstein worked at whitehouse and him and buddy Bill went jetting around up to no good.

Wonder if rappers are pedophiles it seems like everyone else is who knows Bill and Harvey et. al.

Think they'd try anything--they seem to have no lines. They are disgusting swine the rapper kind.

Weinstein and Clinton at the Whitehouse---jetting on Lolita Express most of the time I guess.

Though going to hell they sure create havoc here for a spell.

HARVEY AND BILL BUILT A PORN ROOM

Harvey and Bill built a porn room in the Whitehouse, can you believe this?

McCain is bitter, confused, prone to tantrums, red faced/fits and legendary public meltdowns.

Disasters: Liberals make decisions on what they WANT, conservatives make decisions on what IS.

Pride in identity is not racist. White people have a right to exist.

We don't care what he says or how he talks. He's fixing what's wrong, that's all folks.

She's famous now, a rock star! Gloating in this newfound notoriety she commits treason/treachery.

Gay pride marches are not about equality but pushing sexual degeneracy. Go to one, you will see.

Enough of the vapid virtue signaling celebtards. We're sure not inspired and you're fired.

DAFT LEFT

Further they get from comedy the more they talk of leftwing politics and the more their ratings plummet.

Trump is the reason for devastating victories right now but you won't hear on fake news shows.

Elementary schools teach reading, writing and respect for evil things.

Liberalism is a mental illness but try adapting to it and you'll get even worse in your psychosis.

Obama set the precedent of abusing executive power so now Trump is killing it with it: wow!

OBAMA SET THE PRECEDENT

"Our politics is more vulnerable to conspiracy theories and outright fabrication". Ok but you lost, we won.

Worst presidents ever: The rise of China started with Clintons and Bush, criminals so clever.

Bush embarrassed himself in a highfalutin speech proving he knew nothin' like when he was leadin'.

She's not just stupid she's an evil clown. Using death and mourning to push her hate of Trump!

Wilson wears a fake cowboy hat, Warren says she's an Indian. Liberals fall on their face, pretendin'.

Even big ranchers don't wear their cowboy hat on TV. You're a fool Frederica, we can finally see.

What a fool to wear the (matching colors) cowboy hats but the evil clown is going down: splat.

WATCH FOR EVIL CLOWNS

Watch out for evil clowns cuz they're not funny/create tragedies but Trump's above it fortunately.

DAFT LEFT

Can you believe this? They hate him because he wants America first and he isn't out to get us.

They pejoratively call us "conspiracy theorists" even though it's all written in their papers first.

Here's the real conspiracy theory: the Russians helped Trump get elected (ridiculous and funny).

George Bush lied us into war on the basis of a fabricated conspiracy theory, what about that?

AND WE THOUGHT CARTER WAS BAD

Jimmy Carter bashed Bush and Obama saying "Americans want populism and voted for Trump".

Renewed respect for Carter: Though wrong he never profiteered personally like the others.

Traitor Frederica Wilson took the death of a soldier and used it to project hate upon our national savior.

She's a "rockstar" cuz she bashed the most sacrosanct thing in this country, a soldier's death?

"Empty barrels": a loudmouth that jumps on bandwagons--she can't debate so race-bates.

The only card the liberal democratic globalist party has is RACE but we have the best, the ACE.

To see a race-baiter with a cowboy hat fall on her face is disgusting but it's ok cuz we're winning.

"Getting the base all riled up cuz it gives short-term tactical advantage"-- sounds more like you Barrack.

This surge of nationalism vs. the rules of global order is racist. Geo W. Bush

DAFT LEFT

"A dangerous trend in western countries away from global engagement" said Bush, the deranged.

"Faith in our governmental institutions has declined"--you think so, wonder why?

News fakes: The gap between what they say we're thinking and the truth gets wider every day.

Feminists hate Milo's slurs against them, but don't mind crude obscenities in front of children?

LEFT WANTS NO-GOD AND HUGE GOV

The left wants no God and huge government. The right wants God and small government.

Wanting giant government and no God is atheistic worship of the state or "statism".

Nov. 4 is the next shoe to drop. Nothing may happen or a lot but if they break in here they'll be shot.

The truth is racist and facts are bigotry. Aren't we sick of this lie, this irresponsible trickery?

1776 type candidates are getting elected everywhere--Trump's won and overcome the scare.

THEY CAN'T STAND US WINNING

We're winning and the old guard can't stand it--they want us going under bondage again, believe it.

Democrats, globalists and liberals are so dumbed and wrong they can't see what's happening!

How could they know, no common sense with money to blow but they forgot God/hell below.

DAFT LEFT

There comes a day, hour, minute when God's had enough and that's called reaping the whirlwind.

God's gonna get em--you must know that. Right conquers wrong so call em out, be bold and valiant!

Those creepy ex presidents huddling together against Trump is a sign of desperation of chumps.

DUMBED BY DOGMA

Dumbed by dogma and buffered by money it's no big surprise when kings fall into a pit or go looney.

It wasn't them it was liberalism IN them. They were weak or dumb enough to buy it, forgive em.

They hate Trump but now the world is following Trump, proving these ingrates are chumps!

All the nations are following him--and what a validation

Antifa: If you attack us we're ready to stack bodies. We've had it with your intellectual immaturities.

Many introverts feeling inferior in a social world end in suicide when they could've had God as Guide.

Because he does the right thing/speaks the truth, we love him: every word rings bells in the land.

Your liberal virtue-signaling friends have become worse, more obdurate. Reject now and get with it.

VIOLENCE AGAINST US IS LEGIT

There's been a legitimization of political violence against conservatives.

Amoral dictator may look sharp and cool but he creates a wasteland of ugliness/untruths.

DAFT LEFT

Things are so nice with high morals but so ugly, fat, dumpy, chaotic, lopsided and smelly if low.

Tyrants throughout history have lusted over global government and the bible laid it out.

Soros vs the Ace: force feeding of culture war by funding groups won't work/blow up in his face.

He's the most reviled and hated but also the most loved and revered president in US history.

I don't wanna be treated good, just fairly. Trump

We love healthy debate but they just reject us--cuz they can't debate, only slogans/making a fuss.

SELF-DEFENSE MECHANISMS AND CONSCIENCE

All animals have self-defense mechanisms and we need our guns or weak are killed by the strong.

Sinners have seared consciences (couldn't care less) but mine stings until I make it righteous.

Ellen a sick freak put down our president Donald Trump! Like he'd ever wanna grace her show, huh.

No lady wants to be pegged by her age. It's as bad as racism so a true gentleman never asks.

Ellen freaky said "bring out the big balloons!" while gawking, mouth agape, at Perry's breasts.

It's not that Ellen's remark was sexist, it's that she's a disgusting globalist anti-Trump witch.

Ellen put down Trump, gaped at a woman's breast, and now plays victim as well ("ME TOO").

DAFT LEFT

Now they finally admit that Donald Trump wasn't in a hotel room with a woman urinating on him.

Soros funded groups suing Trump/Alex Jones 1000x, but we're a public aware of these fiends.

"Ok, it was all made up" CNN, NBC, ABC
Russian Hoax by Same Folks

We're not devil worshippers. We're into green pastures, happiness, freedom.

They put us down and called us crazy idiots--for 8 years we took that s*t so rest, music, be starlit.

He already got defeated so now claims he "died at the Alamo" or so the saying goes.

MANUAL UNLEARNS DEMORALIZATION

This manual can help anyone cuz we've all been tainted by the same thing: deliberate demoralization.

Don't get down in the dirt and debate about the "evil" founders. Just say "you're a bore".

I don't have to defend the founders to know what a brilliant document this is, it's kept us free.

Americana was decency minding it's own business. People are busybodies but moral/orderly/happy.

They sexualized five year olds! They taught them homo techniques, they were debauched and bold.

Trump's the first breath of fresh air in over a decade. Decency, Christianity, standing up to bullies.

Trump is just winning, winning, winning. Satan's armies have fallen and it's a brand new inning.

DAFT LEFT

"LGBTQ youth deserve to see their lives depicted on their favorite shows" so we're all debased to low.

The Golden Girls gave us a warped view of glamorous aging.

It's a CULT of not having to think and just joining it. "I'm an intellectual"--just repeating that.

That woman who got rich selling American uranium is all for pedophiles, trannies, gays and lesbians.

True peace requires the presence of justice not just absence of conflict. N.K. Jemisin

FAKE RUSSIAN COLLUSION IS ALL THEY HAVE

The only person NOT involved with Russia is Donald Trump and that's why they want him out.

Liberal minority applauds removing statues/dissing anthem: we're at peace but they create mayhem.

George Washington sacrificed so much to deliver our country to us but we recall him only with a diss.

A tiny minority, a far left radical group. But they're pushing anyway and we let em: so uncool.

Just as America got dirty in the 70's they were also schooled to be social--it's like group complicity.

In the 80's the nerd, the isolate/monastic saint was seen as an hideous outlaw not just quaint.

It was all a setup for communism: commune-ism, and I hated having to adapt to this/also feminism.

Just as all moral lines were dissolved the social became most important: both areas were involved.

DAFT LEFT

It was the contagion of madness, pure and simple. That's how the brain works/they wanna mingle.

They don't realize how transparent they are. Neurosis comes right out, embarrassing to stars.

The only way to deal with moral breakdown into nihilism is by-the-book puritanical rules/thinking.

The Puritans who founded America hated sexual debauchery and that reaction started this country.

Our Puritan beginnings laid the basis for two centuries of relative peace, civility and decency.

We are so far from decency and common sense they actually see Donald Trump as a weird dunce.

TRUMP RANG MY BELL—SAVE US FROM HELL!

Trump rang my bell immediately. I was catapulted to the galaxy with this echo of brighter days.

With male alcoholics a bond with buddies supersedes loyalty to wives--that's the most brutal type.

Evil gets good at denying it exists, but when good stands up evil exits.

Evil hates good cuz losers hate the truth.

Ten thousand more pedophiles arrested! But you'd never know it cuz fake news won't report it.

There is no limit to the violence the left will use to gain control. Look at history: millions gone.

Put a weak woman in power & as the wicked take over lives will change forever/get worse every hour.

The intolerant use our tolerance against us.

DAFT LEFT

Hollywood is politics for good looking people and better actors.

They live in dream notions rather than reality. Like I don't wanna see what's in your trash, silly.

Look at what IS, not what you WANT it to be. NOW make decisions silly

Leftists live in utopia and on that basis they tyrannize over ya

"He's gay, so it's ok".

Hollywood perverts wanna run education or sexualize children, now we see these liberal vermin.

The gay mafia was the Hollywood in-club and how they hated deplorables and middle America.

We should have old fashioned men and women who should be mad not taking donations for the cad.

PEDOPHILIA REFLECTS ABORTION CULTURE

Social adaptation/acculturation: you start to think well, if this is how it is I'll let it all go too.

When friends or family turn against you it hurts the most--all political, occurring from coast to coast.

When a beautiful woman yells a gross shout she's like a flashing jewel in a pig's snout: no clout.

Since pedophilia reflects abortion culture mass arrests will bring refocus and make that matter.

Sin shows and you see it in the effects of illicit sex, like a hex.

Insanity: 50% of millennials would like to live in a communist country.

Without safeguards, government naturally becomes corrupt. It's just it's nature to obstruct.

DAFT LEFT

Popularity has nothing to do with truth. Wanting attention and many friends is all about the youth.

As bad as things get, always remember good overcomes evil--relieving stress over all those people.

I can't take it anymore! Constant bad news when life's so amazing: what a bore--close that old door.

When weak we act out other people's thoughts and habits. To avoid this regression, get strong.

When things don't work do not relapse into cultural images for approval-- these need removal.

UNDERSTANDING LOST IN LOGORHEA (MANY WORDS)

They're so sophisticated you don't know you're being programmed and it's all entirely planned.

I'm no more for Carly--she supported turncoat Megyn Kelly and went against Trump our only ally.

They misunderstand cuz it's all lost in the superfluity of words. Terse verse is all that works.

Vanity, futility, lies: it's all about the ME generation and we see the bad results in the family as it dies.

By seeking stardom they became uppity. Whereas they used to be bubbly now they just act snooty.

They're so full of themselves it makes me sick. In these tragic days they're hip but thick as a brick.

Wimps say "there is nothing that can be done, see?" Meanwhile they want some more for free.

Can they get any more vain and self-involved? It's embarrassing--have we really evolved?

DAFT LEFT

If you're always defending yourself in that particular group you must either repent, exit or have a coup.

Promiscuous, frivolous, destructive and inane: In these things there is no gain, they only drain (a bane).

It wasn't until after he got in that we realized all these things, so now the ol' liberty bell loudly rings.

When I was a feminist I was sickening. They all are when they take that narrative, a deadening.

CONSERVATIVES SEE THROUGH

As a conservative you'll see through everyone you ever knew. They were all taken in but not you.

Allowing them to define you, you don't know who you are. Now go within, repent of sin and be a star.

The best are trivialized in family and herd. They are scoffed at, walked on, dismissed or slurred.

Pictures, pictures and more pictures of themselves smiling. Sickening, it's all about social climbing.

Since "how not to be rejected or criticized" is their whole thing, of course they end alone or in a fling.

Don't make people bigger than they are, for people-obsessions get bizarre (sending many to the bar).

Free market with constitutional rights: that made us most prosperous but so easily gone is that light.

GOVERNMENT THE DANGEROUS MASTER

DAFT LEFT

TYRANNY: Warrantless wire taps, open borders, dictatorial government, IRS taking bank accounts, persecution for political beliefs and funding radical terrorist organizations, government grabbing *everything*.

FREEDOM: private property, free market system, due process, personal rights, high defense, freedom of speech and religion.

BODY OF A JOCKEY

I'm anorexogenic meaning I do best with the body of a jockey and it's called extreme ectomorphy.

I'm not worried about fruit, sugar or white rice cuz I know we run on glucose which fruit/starch is.

I've reached the life phase where it's all work spotted with catnaps. It's a life of luxury to an isolate.

I was banned from a diet group cuz I said we should all just skip dinner. That was like a sin to an eater.

I carb up in the morning with fruits and starches then fast the rest of the day so I can rest the best.

Why would you eat at night before sleep? You eat in the morning to fuel the tank before work, see?

DAILY FASTING IS NOT ANOREXIA

The woman freaked out when I said to skip dinner. In her mind it's normal but where's it written sir?

Juice has the calories and sugar to sustain minus the digestive burps, acid-reflux and pains!

I had digestive problems even as a baby. Being sustained by juice without digestion is a vacation, truly.

Even as a baby food came back up. The body recognized the obstruction to good health and ejected it.

DAFT LEFT

As an adult I'm able to digest but the acid-reflux, the burping and other pains is not worth it.

Sufferers of acid reflux wanna lean on proton inhibitors but I refuse this kinda thing, psychosis-makers.

I live in a hot climate, my own office. I keep it toasty or cool depending, where all my animals are happiest.

A true writer doesn't care about the money he just wants to be read. That's true of me too and it's sad.

So they gyped you, everything comes back to the saint doubled for being troubled and anointed.

100 KAREN KELLOCK BOOKS

AFFINITY OR MISERY
AGELESS CORNUCOPIA
AMERICA AWAKE!
AMERICA'S DAFT ERA
ARTS OF PALEO FASTING
AUTOPHAGY ON CHEATERS
BACKSTABBING NEUROTICS
BETRAYAL TRAUMA
BOOMERS AND BROKENNESS
BOOT ON NECK
CHAMPION GUIDES
COMMIE NUTHOUSE
COMMIES
COMMUNIST SPIRIT
CONTAGION OF MADNESS
CONTAGIOUS MADNESS
CULTURE CLASH BASHED
DAFT LEFT
DAILY FASTARIAN
DAM RATS
DIVERSITY IS CRUELTY
E-RACE WHITE
EVIL FREAKS (Beyond Gross)
THE END OR A BEND?
FEMALE BULLIES AND FEMI-NAZIS
FEMALE CARNALITY
FEMALE DUMB DOWN
FEMALE POWER DRIVE
FEMINISM AND RUIN 1 & 2
FIX FOR MISFITS
FOOLS & TRAMPS
FREEDOM SPEAKING
FRENEMY ENABLER
FRENEMY LIAR
FRENEMY THIEF
FRENEMY TRAITOR
TRENEMY TYRANT
GENIUS IS HELD DOWN
GLOBALISLAM
GOD USES THE FLAWED
HAZE OF THE LATTER DAYS

KAREN KELLOCK PH.D.

M.S. Political Science, San Diego State. Ph.D. in Psychology, University of California Irvine. Postdoctoral: UCI School of Medicine, Dept. of Psychiatry [NIMH Grants]. Developed the Debris Theory of Disease, a theory of system pathology in 120 books and 22 textbooks for the general public. The theory has a general formula: All disease is obstruction, all recovery is elimination, all success is attraction. The three obstructions are people, habit and food. Remove obstruction and snap to your goals, waiting in the wings.